somebody
left

the door
open

Marcia
Bennett

by
Marcia Allen Bennett
illustrations: Joan Dunlap

ISBN: 0-945199-24-4
Second Edition

Illustrations: Joan Dunlap

Book Design: Dorey Schmidt

Journeypark Press
Box 7 Cypress Point
Woodcreek, TX 78676

This book is dedicated

to my grandchildren

who never fail to delight & inspire me.

SOMEBODY

Somebody left the back door open
And let in a bunch of bugs.
Somebody spilled some orange juice
All over our brand new rug.
Somebody messed up the kitchen,
There's ketchup on the floor.
Somebody moved my shoes and sox
And left an apple core.
We can't go anywhere in the car—
Somebody lost the key.
Somebody seems to be everywhere!
I think that somebody is me.

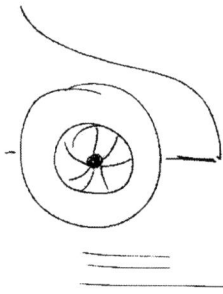

MY CAT AND MY DOG

My cat is named Rover;

He barks and he growls.

My dog, named Miss Kitty, meows.

My dog climbs up trees,

And my cat chases cars,

And they both sleep

On top of my house.

MY TEACHER, MISS FILLYWIG

My teacher, Miss Fillywig,

Reads books backwards;

She adds two and two and gets three.

She tells us that Boston is in California

And that your brain is found in your knee.

Miss Fillywig jumps rope while she calls the roll,

Her ponytails bounce up and down;

Tuesday through Thursday she wears purple jeans,

On Friday, an evening gown.

She is the best teacher I ever had

She says teaching's easy as pie

But Miss Fillywig, we're told,

Won't be teaching next year;

And I cannot figure out why!

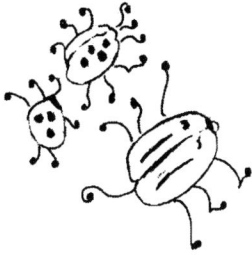

MY STORY

My teacher said,

"Write a story;

Keep it short."

So I did.

This is it.

AMANDA SCHOLASTIC

When Amanda Scholastic got a picnic basket
To take bread and water to school,
We said, "That thing won't hold water!"
She said, "Well, it oughta—but the water just
Goes right on through!"

UPSIDE-DOWN SANDRA

Upside-down Sandra

Has learned how to stand on her

Head for twenty-four hours;

As she waves with her feet

To her friends in the street,

She nibbles on green lemon sours.

CULLEN

My little brother, Cullen,

Can already read. You see

That's pretty special

Since he's only three.

Dad tells him, "Good for you, son.

You'll grow up to be

A scientist or a surgeon;

How proud we'll all be."

My mom and aunts and uncles

All say, "Yes, we agree."

Sometimes I wish someone

Would say those things to me.

CINNAMON SUE

Cinnamon Sue has a wacky hairdo

Like a mushroom on top of her head;

Smeared with cinnamon and butter

She then wonders what her

Hair would taste like on some bread!

SARA'S BREAKFAST

When Sara sits down

Each morning for breakfast,

She cannot decide what to eat:

Pancakes, or waffles, or bacon and eggs

Or maybe some leftover meat

Or breakfast tacos or oatmeal and juice

Or maybe some French-toasted bread.

When she finally decides

What food she will eat

It's time to go back to bed.

SAVANNAH BANANA

Savannah Banana's table manners

Are the strangest that I've ever seen.

With a fork in one hand she's eating her soup

With another, she's eating ice cream.

She uses her knife to eat carrots and beans

While pouring some salt in her tea,

She uses a spoon for eating fried chicken

And her fingers for eating a pea.

She puts chocolate sauce on her mashed potatoes

And spaghetti sauce over her pie.

She likes stewed tomatoes

Stirred up in her milk

And oysters on pancakes (piled high).

She uses her napkin to crumble her cornbread

Beating hard on it with both her fists.

Is this starting to bore you

Or would you like more?

I could go on and on with this list!

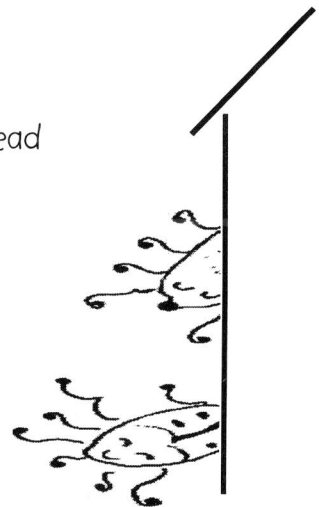

DIGITAL DANNY

Digital Danny keeps up with the time,

He likes to hear bells and alarms.

He wears a cuckoo clock around his neck

And forty watches on each of his arms.

He carries a sundial in his backpack

And if somebody asks him the time,

He says, "Just a moment while I unpack,

But I'm guessing it's quarter to nine."

He pulls out the sundial and sets it all up

And gets mad when it won't give the time;

— We tell him and tell him and tell him again

It won't work if the sun doesn't shine.

JULIA PECULIAR

Julia Peculiar; watch out, she will fool ya'

With her hair hanging over her face.

Is she going or coming?

Is it this way or that?

I hope she won't ask me to race!

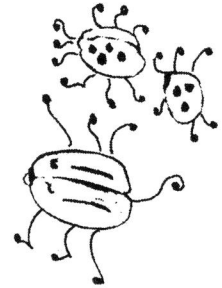

WEIRDLY ZOT THOMAS

Weirdly Zot Thomas wears his pajamas

To swim in the pool or the sea;

Then he goes to the movies

In swim trunks to prove he's

Sillier than you or than me.

JONATHAN MEDIC

Jonathan Medic plans on being a doctor;

When asked what he would like best,

He says, "I'll only take care of sick fingernails.

Other doctors can do all the rest."

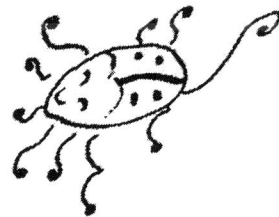

TIMOTHY TUMBLE

Timothy Tumble can't seem to stay still
He moves in his sleep like a busy windmill.
When he's awake the whole house will shake,
It's Timothy, not an earthquake.
Books won't stay on the shelf,
Pictures fall off the wall;
And can you believe that the dining chairs all
Have seat belts so that the family can eat
Without being thrown from their seats?

Timothy jumps upside down on the couch;
Sometimes he falls, but he never says ouch;
And he never gets tired, but the rest of us do
Watching Timothy tumble the whole long day through.

WOULD YOU LIKE TO SLEEP
IN AN OLD MAN'S BEARD?

No, no, no!
I do not want to sleep in my *bed* tonight!

Where would you like to sleep tonight?

Would you like to sleep in an old man's beard?
No, no, no!
It's too scratchy.

Would you like to sleep in a bowl of pudding?
No, no, no!
It's too squishy.

Would you like to sleep in a jar of pickles?
No, no, no!
They're too sour.

Would you like to sleep in an old tin can?

No, no, no!

I can't fit in.

Would you like to sleep on a big round ball?

No, no, no!

Too roly-poly.

Would you like to sleep at the bottom of the sea?

No, no, no!

Too many fishes.

Would you like to sleep on two snowflakes?
No, no, no!
They're too icy.

Would you like to sleep on a seesaw?
No, no, no!
It's too wobbly.

Would you like to sleep in a waterfall?
No, no, no!
It's way too wet!

Would you like to sleep in a grandfather clock?
No, no, no!
It's too ding-dongy.

Would you like to sleep on a pile of rocks?
No, no, no!
They're too lumpy.

Would you like to sleep in a garbage truck?
No, no, no!
It's too smelly.

Would you like to sleep on a pyramid?

No, no, no!

It's much too pointy.

Would you like to sleep in a flock of ducks?

No, no, no!

They're too quacky.

Would you like to sleep in Grandma's
purse?
No, no, no!
Too much junk in there.

Would you like to sleep in
a barber chair?
No, no, no!
Too much hair.

Would you like to
sleep on a red balloon?
No, no, no!
It might go "pop."

Would you like to sleep on a pile of feathers?
No, no, no!
Cause feathers tickle.

Would you like to sleep in a bucket of worms?
No, no, no!
They're too squirmy.

Would you like to sleep on a big bass drum?
No, no, no!
My ears would hurt.

Would you like to sleep on a ceiling fan?
No, no, no!
I'd get dizzy spinning around.

Would you like to sleep on an elephant?
No, no, no!
I might fall off.

Would you like to sleep on the moon or a star?
No, no, no!
That's way too far.

Well then, where would you like to sleep tonight?

I guess I'll sleep in my very own bed.

DO I HAVE TO GO TO CHURCH TODAY?

We go to church on Sundays;
We never miss a service.
I wiggle and I twist and mom asks,
"Why are you so nervous?"

It's just that it's so boring
And so long for little boys,
I'd rather be home playing
With my favorite toys.

So I count the organ pipes,
One hundred sixty-seven,
I guess they need all those
To make the music go to heaven.

I stare at stained glass windows
And pretend I'm in those colors,
Smelling, tasting, touching,
Reds and blues and greens and yellows.

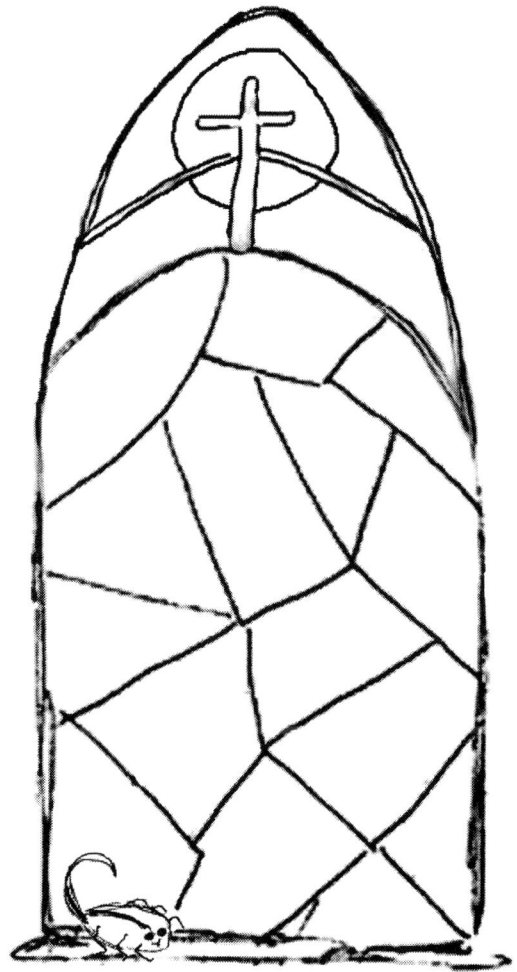

One time while folks were praying,
I crawled beneath the pews
And popped up before the preacher.
He didn't look amused.

"Young man," he said to me
As I looked down at my feet,
"Would you please be so kind
As to return to your seat."

I like it when we sing the songs,
And as I sing each verse
I wonder why they call them "hims"
And never call them "hers."

One Sunday I took a mirror,
Just a little one, you see;
When I pulled it out I made
A great discovery.

If I held that mirror just right
And moved it all around
I could make a little sunbeam dance
And never make a sound.

I lighted up the ceiling,
And the organ and its keys;
I put bright spots on the choir's robes,
They looked like Christmas trees.

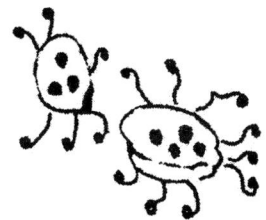

I made a *big* mistake, though,
Not one bit smart or wise:
I shined that little mirror light
Straight in the preacher's eyes.

He stopped right then and looked at me
That look was very long.
And that was when I knew for sure
That what I'd done was wrong.

I was so embarrassed
And knew my folks were, too.
I wished that there had been a hole
For me to drop into!

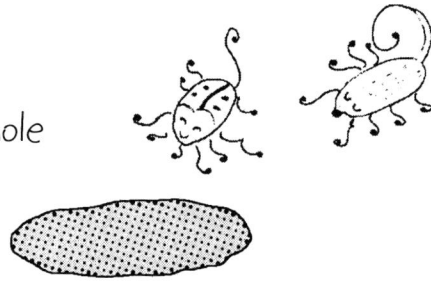

I wished that I could disappear
 Or at least could run and hide.
Maybe I could sneak out
Through that big door on the side.

But Dad grabbed onto my hand
And held it tight and said,
"You must apologize, son.
What you did was pretty bad."

I looked up at the preacher and said
"I'm sorry," and I meant it.
He said, "I forgive you
And I'm glad you have repented.

"I see you understand the message
That was in my talk today.
God forgives us of our wrongs
And loves us anyway."

So that's what it was all about!
We have to say we're sorry.
I guess I'll have a talk with God
And tell him not to worry.

I'll promise not to squirm so much,
And I'll do my very best
To be real good and quiet
And nice and all the rest.

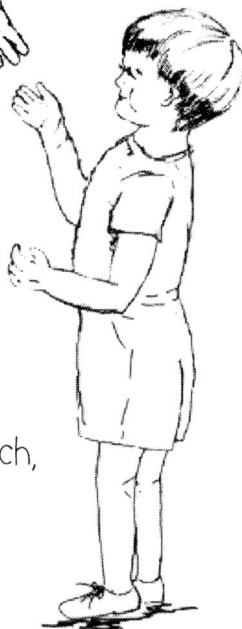

If I need to wiggle,
I'll ask my folks' permission
And when the preacher starts to talk,
I think I'll start to listen!

COUSIN SAM

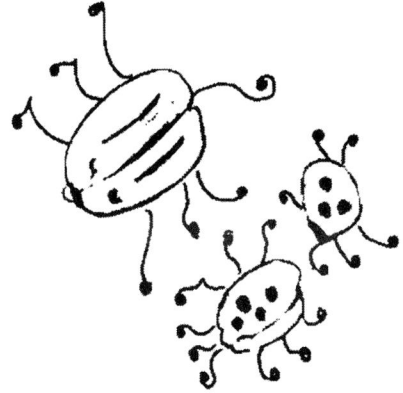

You'd think Cousin Sam,

Would be super clean,

He stays in the bathtub so long.

He throws in some soap

And some little toy boats

And a real ugly plastic King Kong.

There are six building blocks

And a frogman who swims,

A rubber duck is in there, of course.

There are pitchers for pouring

And cups for dipping

And a cowboy who's riding a horse.

There's stuff to make bubbles

And things to make splashes

And a washcloth with a green-colored border,

But Sam never gets clean

Cause he hates to get wet

And won't let his mom put in water!

CLARA VON SNUFFLY

Said Clara Von Snuffly
"My nose is all stuffy;
I must have some awful disease.
My throat is sore,
My eyes are all red
And I'm trying my best not to sneeze."

"I know how to cure that,"
Said Irma Cantu,
"Put your head down between your
        knees."
"No, no," said Lou Simon,
"That's for fainting. For a cold
Eat potatoes and cheese."
"I know what will cure it,"
said Abigail Lee,
"Stand in snow on a hill in a breeze."
"How silly," said Clara,
"In the middle of winter?
I think that I probably would freeze.
I thank you for helping,
I know you mean well
But I'll do what works best for me.
I'll eat a jawbreaker
And lots of ice cream
And drink some peppermint tea."

BEN SOLARPLEXUS

Ben Solarplexus, my friend from West Texas,

Wears his cowboy boots on his hands.

That way, he explains,

Whenever it rains

They don't get messed up with wet sand.

ALICIA PATRICIA

AliciaPatriciaKimberlyKate

ElizabethHeatherDupree

AllisonSaraMariaSue has

The *shortest* name in her family.

HARRIET HOLIDAY

Harriet Holiday takes harp lessons

Is she studying to be an angel or what?

She thinks that she's playing like an angel already

But I'll tell you a secret—she's not!

VANILLA McFEE

Vanilla McFee

Goes to school in a tree

And does all her studying there.

When I asked her why

She said, "'Cause it's high

And I'm sure that the tree doesn't care."

E-MAIL ERNIE

Whenever I go to Ernie's to play,

He says importantly,

"Gotta go check my e-mail."

He gets off the school bus

Then turns and he shouts,

"Gotta go check my e-mail."

When we're talking on the phone,

He never says goodbye, it's

"Gotta go check my e-mail."

One night at dinner at Ernie's house

Right in the middle of pizza, he said,

"Gotta go check my e-mail."

I quietly followed

And peeked in his room.

There's no computer here, I thought,

Just a parakeet in a big cage.

Then Ernie stepped up to the cage

with a smile on his face, and he said,

"Hi, there, E-mail. Are you hungry?"

Hi E mail

ALISTAIR

Some little kids have blankets

They carry everywhere.

Others have a stuffed toy

Like a bunny or a bear

But it sure does get to be a pain

With my brother Alistair

Cause everywhere we ever go

He takes his rocking chair.

VERNA VOLUME

Verna Volume carries books

Everywhere she goes:

Thin books and thick books

Orange books and green books

Pop-up books, dictionaries

Fancy books and ordinary

In her arms and on her head

In her backpack, pockets full

Of books and books and books and books...

Books from libraries, books from malls

Books on building barns with stalls

Books with pictures, books with none

Books on how to cook seaweed—

It would make more sense to me

If Verna just knew how to read.

JUDITH A. TITUS

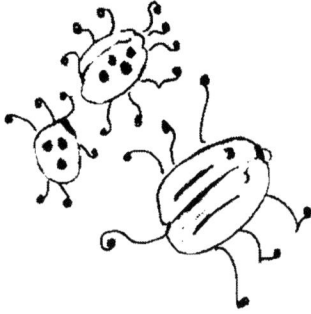

Judith A. Titus has telephonitus,

I think the phone's stuck on her ear;

She talks to her friends

And her aunts and her uncles

And the lady who's feeding reindeer.

She calls up a fellow who lives down in...

"Hello, would you speak louder so I can hear?"

And she chats with a man who is driving a van

Of old ladies out to the fair.

She telephones Russia, and Europe, and China

And six people who live in Lapland.

She gabs with the vet

Who is treating her pet

Anaconda. "You say he'll be fine?"

Judith never hangs up, she just

Punches more numbers

To talk to more people, you see.

It's hard to believe, but I've waited six years

And Judith has never called me!

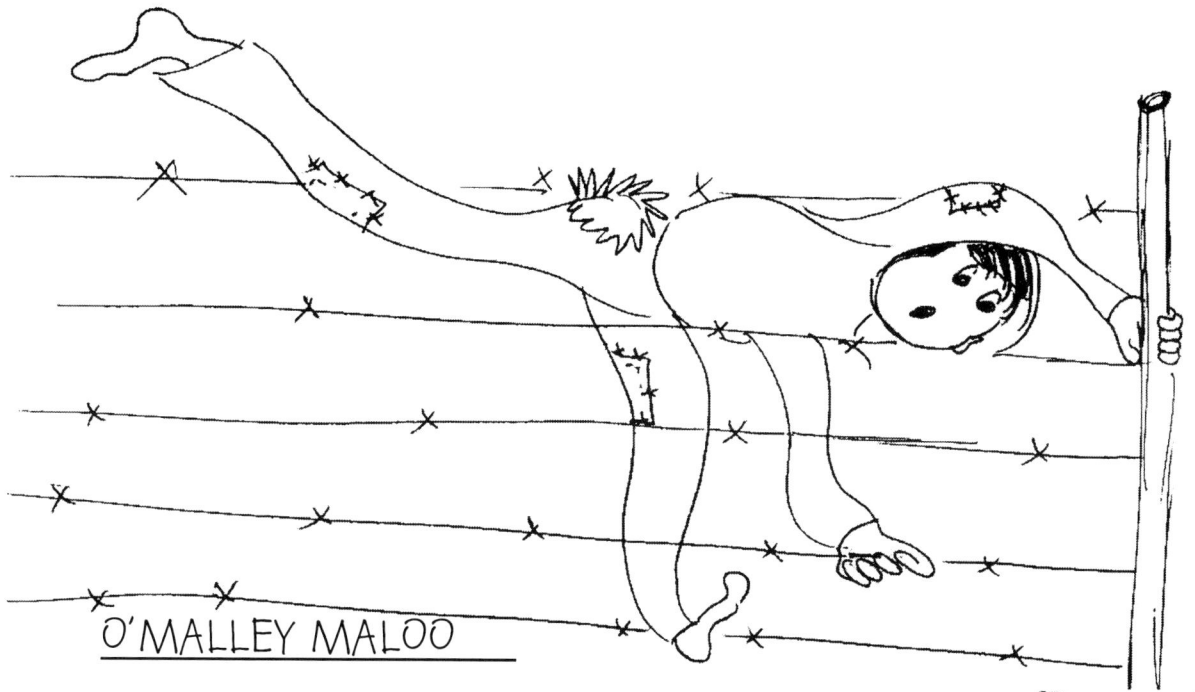

O'MALLEY MALOO

He climbs barbed-wire fences, that O'Malley Maloo

Right behind is his sister, Kachoo.

When Maloo rips his britches

Kachoo puts in some stitches

And Maloo's britches are 'most good as new.

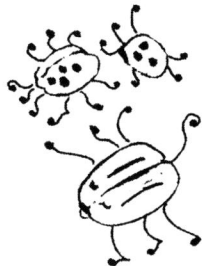

CAROLYN CADILLAC

Carolyn Cadillac likes toy cars

She keeps them in boxes and jars;

She piles them in closets

On floors and on carpets

And pokes them into candy bars.

Cars hang from her ceiling

Like colorful spiders

Waiting to drop from the skies,

Cars are inside her purse

And what's even worse

She bakes them in cakes and in pies.

There's a jeep in her soup

And a truck in her spinach,

Ten fire engines are in her bed.

She even has tractors

And 18-wheel semis.

She sleeps with those under her head.

FRIENDS GETTING AROUND

Sara hops up the street,

Jose slides down the hill,

While Christopher crawls on his belly.

Susie slithers around

Like a snake on the ground.

Martin waddles

And eats toast and jelly.

COLORFUL JOHN

John started out to school one day

With one red sock and one green.

His mom said, "John, your socks don't match.

They really do look pretty bad."

John looked down at his colorful feet,

He thought for a moment and said,

"They look kind of funny, but I don't care.

I'll just start a new fad." And he did!!

WIMBERLEY WILLIE

Wimberley Willie is a good friend of mine,

I see him when I go to town.

He wears dirty clothes

And refuses to shave and his

Hair hangs almost to the ground.

He plays a guitar and sings off Key,

He's a man some people can't stand.

But I like old Willie, he talks to me

And shakes hands like I'm a grown man.

Marcia Allen Bennett raised four children, then went looking for more as an elementary teacher and librarian. After retiring with her husband Bill to Wimberley in the Texas Hill country, her pastimes have included woodcarving, building folk instruments such as a mountain dulcimer, hammered dulcimer and Irish harp, and playing them. She has been honored by the International Guild of Miniature Artisans for her work in creating miniature furniture. This is her second children's book.

Joan Dunlap's interest in drawing began when she was a child. Her career, however, was that of a primary teacher of pre-school and kindergarten. When she retired, she resumed her art, and became noted for her realistic portraits of animals. For this, her first children's book illustrations, she created imaginative, jolly and carefree characters which echo the humor of Bennett's poems. Dunlap lives in Wimberley with her husband.